William H Porter

Spiritual Longings and Divine Reponses

William H Porter

Spiritual Longings and Divine Reponses

ISBN/EAN: 9783337333928

Printed in Europe, USA, Canada, Australia, Japan

Cover: Foto ©Lupo / pixelio.de

More available books at **www.hansebooks.com**

PREFACE

This little volumn was suggested by a sermon of C. H. Spurgeon, from the text "Deep calleth unto deep." Ps. 42 : 7. Subject—"The deeps in God answering to the deeps in man."

It was prepared and published at the request of Mr. F. Heath, Secretary Y. M. C. A., London, Ont., for the use of christians and christian workers.

Among the many who have encouraged and aided the publication of this little work special mention should be made of Rev. D. McGillivray, (Pres.), London, and T. S. Shenston, Esq., and Mr. A. Harris, Brantford.

Its preparation has been a "work of faith and labor of love."

The unexpected favor it has met with encourages the publication of this second enlarged edition.

And now with the prayer " O send out thy light and thy truth," it is trustingly sent forth by the

AUTHOR.

DEDICATION

Unto Him that is able to do exceeding abundantly above all that we ask or think, according to the power that worketh in us, unto Him be the glory in the church by Christ Jesus, throughout all ages, world without end. Amen. Eph. 3: 20, 21.

MY SAVIOUR.

Dear Saviour, may I call thee mine?
   My hope, my friend, my guide?
Perish in ruins all that would
   With thee my heart divide.
My Saviour's pard'ning voice I'd hear,
   His saving pow'r adore,
And have his love and zeal inspire
   My own yet more and more.

My Saviour's hallow'd cross I'd bear,
   Who bore the cross for me,
And who in shameful agony
   Expired upon the tree.
My Saviour's lowly mind I'd have,
   Ambitious thoughts at rest,
And walking in his heav'nly ways
   Be with his presence blest.

My Saviour's arm I'd lean upon,
   His power alone I'd prove;
And knowing only his sweet will,
   I'd prompt to duty move.
My Saviour's loving words I'd hear,
   His wondrous works I'd trace,
Till called to dwell forever near
   And gaze upon his face.

W. H. PORTER.

SPIRITUAL LONGINGS

—AND—

Divine Responses.

LONGING AFTER GOD.

As the hart panteth after the water brooks, so panteth my soul after thee, O God. My soul thirsteth for God. Ps. 42 : 1, 2. *My heart and my flesh crieth out for the living God.* 84 : 2.

TO FIND GOD.

God hath made of one blood all nations of men, that they should seek the Lord, if haply they might feel after him and find him, though he be not far from every one of us. Acts 17 : 26, 27.

Oh, that I knew where I might find him! Job 23 : 3.

Seek ye the Lord while he may be found, call ye upon him while he is near. Is. 55:6.

With my soul have I desired thee in the night; yea, with my spirit within me will I seek thee early. Is. 26: 9.

Ye shall call upon me, and go and pray unto me; and ye shall seek me, and find me, when ye shall search for me with all your heart. Jer. 29: 12, 13.

By night on my bed I sought him whom my soul loveth; I sought him, but I found him not. I will rise now and go about the city, in the streets, and in the broad ways I will seek him whom my soul loveth. Cant. 3: 1, 2.

Thou shall find him if thou seek him with all thy heart, and with all thy soul Deut. 4: 29.

TO SEE GOD.

Blessed are the pure in heart for they shall see God.—Matt. 5: 8.

Verily thou art a God that hidest thyself; O God of Israel, the Saviour. Is. 54:15.

No man hath seen God at any time; the only begotten Son, who is in the bosom of the Father, he hath declared him. John 1: 18.

Behold, I go forward, but he is not there; and backward, but I cannot perceive him; on the left hand, where he doth work, but I cannot behold him; he hideth himself on the right hand, that I cannot see him. Job 23: 8, 9.

He that hath my commandments, and keepeth them, he it is that loveth me; and he that loveth me shall be loved of my father, and I will love him, and will manifest myself to him. John 14: 21.

I know that my redeemer liveth, and that he shall stand at the latter day upon the earth; and though after my skin worms destroy this body, yet in my flesh shall I see God; whom I shall see for myself, and mine eyes shall behold, and not another; though my reins be consumed within me. Job 19, 25-27. For now we see through a glass darkly, but then face to face. 1 Cor. 13: 12.

TO KNOW GOD.

Let not the wise man glory in his wisdom, neither let the mighty man glory in his might; let not the rich man glory in his riches, but let him that glorieth glory in this, that he understandeth and knoweth me saith the Lord. Jer. 9:23, 24.

The world by wisdom knew not God. 1 Cor. 1:21.

My people shall know my name. Is. 52, 6. I will give them a heart to know me. Jer. 24:7.

This is life eternal, that they might know thee, the only true God, and Jesus Christ, whom thou hast sent. John 17:3.

Everyone that loveth is born of God, and knoweth God, for God is love. 1 John 4:7.

I count all things but loss for the excellency of the knowledge of Christ Jesus my Lord. Phil. 3:8.

Grow in grace, and in the knowledge of our Lord and Saviour Jesus Christ. 2 Pet. 3:18.

We know that the Son of God is come, and hath given us an understanding that we may know him that is true. 1 John 5:20.

Grace and peace be multiplied unto you through the knowledge of God, and of Jesus our Lord. 2 Pet. 1:2.

TO BE NEAR GOD.

It is good for me to draw near to God.—Ps. 73: 28.

O God, be not far from me. Ps. 71, 12.

Now in Christ Jesus, ye who sometimes were far off, are made nigh by the blood of Christ. Eph. 2, 13. For the law made nothing perfect, but the bringing in of a better hope did ; by the which we draw nigh to God. Heb. 7 : 19.

O Lord, draw near unto my soul. Ps. 71 : 18.

Draw nigh to God, and he will draw nigh to you. Jas. 4: 8. The Lord is nigh unto them that are of a broken heart. Ps. 34: 18. The Lord is nigh unto all them that call upon him, to all them that call upon him in truth. 145: 18.

Thou art near, O Lord. Ps. 119: 151.

Ye have seen how I bare you on eagles' wings, and brought you unto myself. Ex. 19: 4.

Having therefore boldness to enter into the holiest by the blood of Jesus. Let us draw near with a true heart, in full assurance of faith. Heb. 10, 19-22. For what nation is there who hath God so nigh unto them, as the Lord our God is in all things that we call upon him for. Deut. 4: 7.

TO BEHOLD HIS BEAUTY AND HIS GLORY.

How great is his beauty.—Zech. 9: 17.

One thing have I desired of the Lord, that will I seek after; that I may dwell in the house of the Lord all the days of my life, to behold the beauty of the Lord, and to enquire in his temple. Ps. 27: 4.

Thine eyes shall see the king in his beauty. Is. 33: 17.

I beseech thee, shew me thy glory. Ex. 33: 18.

God, who commanded the light to shine out of darkness, hath shined in our hearts, to give the light of the knowledge of the glory of God in the face of Jesus Christ. 2 Cor. 4: 6.

O God, thou art my God; early will I seek thee: my soul thirsteth for thee; my flesh longeth for thee in a dry and thirsty land where no water is; to see thy power and thy glory, so as I have seen thee in the sanctuary. Ps. 63: 1, 2.

Father, I will that they also whom thou hast given me, be with me where I am; that they may behold my glory. John 17: 24.

TO BE WITH AND LIKE GOD.

They shall see his face; and his name shall be in their foreheads. Rev. 22: 4.

Surely in what place my Lord the king shall be, even there also will thy servant be. 2 Sam. 15: 21.

Where I am, there shall also my servant be. John 12: 26.

Whilst we are at home in the body, we are absent from the Lord. We are willing rather to be absent from the body and to be present with the Lord. 2 Cor. 5: 6. 8. Having a desire to depart, and to be with Christ, which is far better. Phil. 1 : 23.

I go to prepare a place or you. And if I go and prepare a place for you, I will come again and receive you unto myself; that where I am there ye may be also. John 14 : 2, 3.

When shall I come and appear before God? Ps. 42 : 2.

When Christ, who is our life, shall appear, then shall ye also appear with him in glory. Col. 3: 4.

Beloved, now are we the sons of God, and it doth not yet appear what we shall be; but we know that when he shall appear, we shall be like him; for we shall see him as he is. 1 John 3 : 2.

GOD'S MERCY.

All the paths of the Lord are mercy. Ps. 25 : 10.

God be merciful to me a sinner. Luke 18 : 33.

Whoso confesseth and forsaketh his sins shall have mercy. Prov. 28 : 13.

Have mercy upon me, O God, according to thy loving kindness; according to the multitude of thy tender mercies blot out my transgressions. Ps. 51 : 1.

Let Israel hope in the Lord; for with the Lord there is mercy, and with him is plenteous redemption. Ps. 130 : 7.

Hear, O Lord, and have mercy upon me. Ps. 30 : 10. For thou, Lord, art good, and ready to forgive, and plenteous in mercy unto all them that call upon thee. 86 : 5.

God is rich in mercy. Eph. 2 : 4. He delighteth in mercy. Mic. 7 : 18

Turn thee unto me, and have mercy upon me; for I am desolate and afflicted. Ps. 25 : 16.

Sing, O heavens, and be joyful, O earth, and break into singing, O mountains; for the Lord hath comforted his people, and will have mercy upon the afflicted Is. 49 : 13.

THE FORGIVENESS OF SIN.

Blessed is he whose transgression is forgiven, whose sin is covered. Ps. 32:11.

I have sinned; what shall I do unto thee, O thou preserver of men? Job 7:20.

Only acknowledge thine iniquity, that thou hast transgressed against the Lord thy God. Jer. 3:13.

If we confess our sins he is faithful and just to forgive us our sins, and to cleanse us from all unrighteousness. 1 John 1:9.

He looketh upon men, and if any say, I have sinned, and perverted that which was right, and it profited me not; he will deliver his soul from going unto the pit, and his life shall see the light. Job 33:27, 28.

And David said unto Nathan, I have sinned against the Lord. And Nathan said unto David, the Lord also hath put away thy sin. 2 Sam. 12:13.

When I kept silence, my bones waxed old through my roaring all day long. For day and night thy hand was heavy upon me. I acknowledge my sin unto thee, and mine iniquity have I not hid. I said, I will confess my transgression unto the Lord; and thou forgavest the iniquity of my sin. Ps. 32:3-5.

FORGIVENESS.

There is forgiveness with thee that thou mayest be feared. Ps. 130:4.

Why dost thou not pardon my transgression, and take away mine iniquity? Job. 7 : 21.

Let the wicked forsake his way, and the unrighteous man his thoughts; and let him return unto the Lord, and he will have mercy upon him; and to our God, for he will abundantly pardon. Is. 55 : 7

For thy name sake, O Lord, pardon mine iniquity for it is great. Ps. 25 : 11.

I, even I, am he that blotteth out thy transgressions, for mine own sake, and will not remember thy sins. Is. 43 : 25.

Hide thy face from my sins, and blot out all mine iniquities. Ps. 51 : 9.

I have blotted out as a thick cloud thy transgressions, and as a cloud thy sins. Is. 44 : 22.

Who is a God like unto thee, that pardoneth iniquity? Mic. 7 : 18. A God ready to pardon. Neh 9 : 17. Thou hast forgiven the iniquity of thy people; thou hast covered all thy sins. Ps. 85 : 2. Thou wilt cast all their sins into the depths of the sea. Mic. 7 : 19. As far as the east is from the west, so far hath he removed our transgression from us. Ps. 103 : 12.

TO BE JUSTIFIED

Blessed is the man unto whom the Lord imputeth not iniquity. Ps. 32:2.

How can man be justified before God? Job. 9 : 2.

He that justifieth the wicked, and he that condemneth the just, both are abomination to the Lord. Prov. 17 : 15. If I justify myself, mine own mouth shall condemn me : if I say I am perfect, it shall prove me perverse. Job 9 : 20. For in many things we all offend. Jas. 3 : 2. If we say that we have no sin, we deceive ourselves, and the truth is not in us. 1 John 1 : 8. For there is not a just man upon earth, that doeth good, and sinneth not. Ecc. 7 : 20. The heart of the sons of men is full of evil. 9 : 3. The heart is deceitful above all things, and desperately wicked, who can know it? Jer. 17 : 9. For the imagination of the thoughts of man's heart is only evil continually. Gen. 6 : 5.

The Lord looked down from heaven upon the children of men, to see if there were any that did understand, and seek God. They are all gone aside, they are together become filthy, there is none that doeth good, no not one. Ps. 14 : 2, 3.

TO BE JUSTIFIED.

For in thy sight shall no man living be justified. Ps. 143 : 2. For we have before proved, both Jews, and Greeks, that they are all under sin. For there is no difference. Now we know that what things soever the law saith, it saith to them that are under the law : that every mouth may be stopped, and all the world may become guilty before God. Therefore by the deeds of the law there shall no flesh be justified in his sight. For all have sinned, and come short of the glory of God.— Rom. 3 : 9, 19, 23.

How then can man be justified with God. Job 25:4. A God of truth, and without iniquity, just and right is he. Deut. 32 : 4. Of purer eyes than to behold evil, and that cannot look on iniquity · Hab. 1 : 13, and that will by no means clear the guilty. Ex- 34 : 7.

Behold, now I have ordered my cause, I know that I shall be justified. Job 13:18.

For he is near that justifieth me. Is. 50 : 8. It is God that justifieth. Rom. 8:33. A just God and a Saviour. 45 : 21. For he hath made him to be sin for us, who knew no sin, that we might be made the righteousness of God in him. 2 Cor. 5 : 21.

TO BE JUSTIFIED.

For Christ also hath once suffered for sins, the just for the unjust, that he might bring us to God. 1 Pet. 3:18. For when we were yet without strength, in due time Christ died for the ungodly. Much more then, being now justified by his blood, we shall be saved from wrath through him. Rom. 5 : 6, 9. Being justified freely by his grace through the redemption that is in Christ Jesus. Whom God hath set forth to be a propitiation, through faith in his blood, to declare his righteousness for the remission of sins that are past through the forbearance of God ; that he might be just and the justifier of him who believeth in Jesus 3:24-26.

Be it known unto you, therefore, that through this man is preached unto you the forgiveness of sins ; and by him all that believe are justified from all things. Acts 13 : 38, 39. For to him that worketh not, but believeth in him that justifieth the ungodly, his faith is counted for righteousness. Rom 4 : 5. Therefore being justified by faith, we have peace with God through our Lord Jesus Christ; through whom we have now received the atonement.—*at-one-ment.* 5 : 1, 11.

TO BE CLEANSED.

Many shall be purified, and made white. Dan. 12:10.

What is man, that he should be clean? Job 15:14. Or how can he be clean that is born of a woman? 25:4. If I wash myself with snow water, and make my hands never so clean. 9:30. Yet shalt thou plunge me in the ditch, and mine own clothes shall abhor me. 9:30, 31. For we are all as an unclean thing, and all our righteousnesses are as filthy rags. Is. 64:6.

Now Joshua was clothed with filthy garments, and stood before the angel. And he answered and spake unto those that stood before him, saying, Take away the filthy garments from him. And unto him he said, Behold, I have caused thine iniquity to pass from thee, and I will clothe thee with change of raiment. Zech. 3:3, 4.

Let us be glad and rejoice, and give honour to him; for the marriage of the Lamb is come, and his wife hath made herself ready. Rev. 19:7.

And to her was granted that she should be arrayed in fine linen, clean and white; for the fine linen is the righteousness of saints. Rev. 19:8.

CLEANSED.

Ye are washed, ye are sanctified. 1 Cor. 6:11.

Who can understand his errors? cleanse thou me from secret faults. Ps. 19:12.

I will sprinkle clean water upon you, and ye shall be clean; from all your filthiness, and from all your idols will I cleanse you. Ez. 36:25.

Purge me with hyssop, and I shall be clean: wash me and I shall be whiter than snow. Ps. 51:7.

Though your sins be as scarlet, they shall be as white as snow; though they be red like crimson, they shall be as wool. Is. 1:18.

Wash me thoroughly from mine iniquity, and cleanse me from my sin. Ps. 51:2.

Christ loved the church and gave himself for it; that he might sanctify and cleanse it with the washing of water by the word. That he might present it to himself a glorious church, not having spot, or wrinkle, or any such thing. Eph. 5:25–27.

CLEANSED.

Now ye are clean through the word which I have spoken unto you. John 15:3.

Create in me a clean heart, O God; and renew a right spirit within me. Ps. 51:10.

A new heart also will I give you, and a new spirit will I put within you. Ez. 36:26.

The blood of Jesus Christ his Son cleanseth us from all sin. 1 John 1:17.

If the blood of bulls and of goats, and the ashes of an heifer sprinkling the unclean, sanctifieth to the purifying of the flesh, how much more shall the blood of Christ, who through the eternal Spirit offered himself without spot to God, purge your conscience from dead works to serve the living God? Heb. 9:13, 14.

What are these which are arrayed in white robes? and whence came they? Rev. 7:13.

These are they which came out of great tribulation, and have washed their robes and made them white in the blood of the Lamb. Rev 7:14

Unto him that loved us, and washed us from our sins in his own blood. To him be glory and dominion for ever and ever. Amen. Rev. 1:5, 6.

PEACE.

God hath called us to peace   1 Cor. 7:15.

There is no peace, saith my God, to the wicked. Is. 48 : 22. The wicked are like the troubled sea, when it cannot rest, whose waters cast up mire and dirt. 57 : 20. The way of peace they know not. 59 : 8.

Acquaint now thyself with him, and be at peace ; thereby good shall come unto thee. Job. 22 : 21.

Lord thou wilt ordain peace for us. Is. 26 : 12.

The Lord will bless his people with peace. Ps. 29 : 11.

He will speak peace unto his people and to his saints. Ps. 85 : 8.

Having made peace through the blood of his cross; Col. 1 : 20. He came and preached peace to you who were afar off, and to them that were nigh. Eph. 2 : 17.

The chastisement of our peace was upon him, and with his stripes we are healed. Is. 53 : 5. For he is our peace. Eph. 2 : 14. Therefore being justified by faith, we have peace with God through our Lord Jesus Christ. Rom. 5 : 1.

Now the God of hope fill you with all joy and peace in believing. Rom. 15 : 13.

PEACE.

Peace I leave with you: my peace I give unto you. John 14:27.

Great peace have they who love thy law; and nothing shall offend them. Ps. 119:165. And all thy children shall be taught of the Lord; and great shall be the peace of thy children. Is. 54:13.

These things have I spoken unto you that in me ye might have peace. John 16:33. O, that thou hadst hearkened to my commandments; then had thy peace been as a river. Is. 48:18.

Thou wilt keep him in perfect peace, whose mind is stayed on thee, because he trusteth in thee. Is. 26:3.

The work of righteousness shall be peace; and the effect of righteousness, quietness and assurance forever. And my people shall dwell in a peaceable habitation, and in sure dwellings, and in quiet resting places. Is. 32:17, 18.

Now the Lord of peace himself gives you peace always by all means. 2 Thess. 3:16. And let the peace of God rule in your hearts, to the which also ye are called. Col. 3:15. For the kingdom of God is not meat and drink, but righteousness, and peace, and joy in the Holy Ghost. Rom. 14:17.

REST.

The Lord shall give thee rest from thy sorrow, and from thy fear, and from thy hard bondage. Is. 14:3.

O Lord our God, we rest on thee, and in thy name we go. 2 Chron. 14:11.

Thus saith the Lord, Stand ye in the ways, and see, and ask for the old paths, where is the good way, and walk therein, and ye shall find rest for your souls. Jer. 6:16.

We who have believed do enter into rest. Heb. 4:3.

Come unto me all ye that labor and are heavy laden, and I will give you rest. Take my yoke upon you, and learn of me; for I am meek and lowly in heart: and ye shall find rest unto your souls. Matt. 11:28, 29.

Return unto thy rest, O my soul; for the Lord hath dealt bountifully with thee. Ps. 116:7.

Arise ye, and depart; for this is not your rest. Mic. 2:10.

O that I had wings like a dove! for then would I fly away, and be at rest. Ps. 55:6.

Blessed are the dead who die in the Lord from henceforth: Yea, saith the Spirit, that they may rest from their labors; and their works do follow them. Rev. 14:13.

GUIDANCE.

He led them forth by the right way, that they might go unto a city of habitation. Ps. 107:7

O Lord, I know that the way of man is not in himself: it is not in man that walketh to direct his steps. Jer. 10:23.

I will bring the blind by a way that they know not; I will lead them in paths that they have not known. Is. 42:16.

Cause me to know the way wherein I should walk, for I lift up my soul unto thee. Ps. 143:8.

I will instruct thee, and teach thee in the way that thou shalt go; I will guide thee with mine eye. Ps. 32:8. I am the Lord thy God who leadeth thee by the way that thou shouldest go. Is. 48:17.

This God is our God, he will be our guide even unto death. Ps. 48:14. Thou shalt guide me with thy counsel, and afterward receive me to glory. Ps. 73:24.

Trust in the Lord with all thine heart; and lean not unto thine own understanding. In all thy ways acknowledge him, and he shall direct thy paths. Prov. 3:5, 6. And thine ears shall hear a word behind thee saying, This is the way, walk ye in it, when ye turn to the right hand, and when ye turn to the left. Is. 30:21.

CHRISTIAN WORK.

Who is willing to consecrate his service this day unto the Lord? 1 Chron. 29 : 5.

Lord, what will thou have me to do. Acts 9 : 6.

Go work to-day in my vine-yard. Mat. 21:28. Whatsoever thy hand findeth to do, do it with thy might. Ecc. 9 : 10. Redeeming the time—*buying up opportunities.* Eph. 5:16. Instant in season, out of season. 2 : Tim. 4 : 2. Steadfast, unmovable, always abounding in the work of the Lord, forasmuch as ye know that your labor is not in vain in the Lord. 1. Cor. 15 : 58.

Lord, and what shall this man do ? John 21 : 21.

What is that to thee ? follow thou me. John 21 : 22. To every man his work. Mark. 13 : 34. Every one over against his own house Neh. 3:28. As every man hath received the gift, even so minister the same one to another, as good stewards of the manifold grace of God. 1 Pet. 4 : 10. And whatsoever ye do, do it heartly, as unto the Lord, and not unto men ; knowing that of the Lord ye shall receive the reward of the inheritance : for ye serve the Lord Christ. Col. 3: 23, 24.

CHRISTIAN WORK.

Not by might, nor by power, but by my Spirit, saith the Lord of hosts. Zech. 4:7.

Who is sufficient for these things. 2 Cor. 2 : 16.

My grace is sufficient for thee ; for my strength is made perfect in weakness. 2 Cor. 12 : 9.

Ah, Lord God ; I cannot speak, for I am a child. Jer. 1 : 6.

Say not, I am a child ; for thou shalt go to all that I shall send thee ; and whatsoever I command thee thou shalt speak. Jer. 1 : 7.

Run, speak to this young man. Zech. 2 : 4. Go home to thy friends, and tell them how great things the Lord hath done for thee. Mark 5 : 19. Go out into the highways and hedges, and compel them to come in, that my house may be filled. Luke 14:23

Lord, I am not eloquent, but I am slow of speech, and of a slow tongue. Ex 4:10.

Who hath made man's mouth? have not I the Lord? Now therefore go and I will be with thy mouth, and teach thee what thou shalt say. Ex. 4 : 11, 12. For I will give you a mouth and wisdom. Luke 21:15. For it is not ye that speak, but the Spirit of your Father that speaketh in you. Matt. 10:20.

CHRISTIAN WORK.

I know thy works, how thou hast borne, and hast patience, and for my name's sake hast labored, and hast not fainted. Rev. 2:2, 3.

Who hath believed our report? and to whom is the arm of the Lord revealed? Is. 53 1.

He that observeth the wind, shall not sow; and he that regardeth the clouds shall not reap. Ecc. 11:4. In the morning sow thy seed, and in the evening withhold not thine hand: for thou knowest not whether shall prosper, either this or that, or whether they both shall be alike good. 6. He that goeth forth and weepeth, bearing precious seed, shall doubtless come again with rejoicing, bringing his sheaves with him. Ps. 126:6.

I have labored in vain, and spent my strength for nought. Is. 49:4.

It is good that a man should both hope, and quietly wait for the salvation of the Lord. Lam. 3:26. Behold the husbandman waiteth for the precious fruit of the earth, and hath long patience for it, until he receive the early and latter rain. Jas. 5:7. Let us not be weary in well doing: for in due season we shall reap, if we faint not. Gal. 6:9.

CHRISTIAN WORK.

Be strong and of a good courage; for the Lord thy God is with thee whithersoever thou goest. Josh. 1 : 19.

Master, we have toiled all night, and have taken nothing; nevertheless, at thy word I will let down the net. Luke 5 : 5.

Cast the net on the right side of the ship, and ye shall find. John 21: 6. He that winneth souls is wise. Prov. 11 : 30. A word in due season, how good it is. 15:23 How forcible are right words. Job 6 : 25. The words of the wise are heard in quiet, more than the cry of him that ruleth among fools. Ecc. 9:17. The words of the wise are as goads, and as nails fastened by the masters of assemblies, which are given from one shepherd. Ecc. 12:11. And they that be wise shall shine as the brightness of the firmament; and they that turn many to righteousness, as the stars forever and ever. Dan. 12:13.

Here am I, send me. Is. 6:8.

As my Father hath sent me, even so send I you. John 20:21.

I will go in the strength of the Lord God: I will make mention of thy righteousness, even of thine only. Ps. 71:16.

Lo, I am with you always, even unto the end of the world. Matt. 28 : 20.

GOD'S WORD.

Thy testimonies are wonderful. Psalm 119 : 129.

Thou hast magnified thy word, above all thy name. Ps. 138 : 2.

I have written to him the great things of my law, but they were counted as a strange thing. Hos. 8 : 12.

INSPIRED.

These be the last words of David, the anointed of God, and the sweet psalmist of Israel. The Spirit of the Lord spake by me, and his word was in my tongue. 2 Sam. 13 : 1, 2.

Speak, Lord, for thy servant heareth. 1 Sam. 3 : 9.

God spake in times past unto the fathers by the prophets. Heb. 1 : 1.

I will hear what God the Lord will speak. Ps. 85 : 8.

God hath spoken by the mouth of all his holy prophets since the world began. Acts 3 : 21. For the prophecy came not in old time by the will of man: but holy men of God spake as they were moved by the Holy Ghost. 2 Pet. 1 : 21.

SPIRITUALLY UNDERSTOOD.

The natural man receiveth not the things of the Spirit of God; for they are foolishness unto him; neither can he know them, because they are spiritually discerned. 1 Cor. 2:14.

Open thou mine eyes, that I may behold wondrous things out of thy law. Ps. 119:18.

Then opened he their understanding, that they might understand the scriptures. Lu. 24:45.

O Lord, teach me thy statutes. Ps. 119:12-26.

The Comforter, who is the Holy Ghost, whom the Father will send in my name, he will teach you all things. John 19:26.

Lead me in thy truth, and teach me. Ps. 25:5.

When he, the spirit of truth, is come, he will guide you into all truth. John 16:13.

That which I see not, teach thou me. Job 34:32.

Ye need not that any one teach you, but the anointing which ye received of him, abideth in you, and teacheth you of all things. 1 John 2:27.

PURE AND PURIFYING.

Every word of God is pure. Prov. 30 : 5.

Thy word is very pure; therefore thy servant loveth it. Ps. 119 : 140

The words of the Lord are pure words; as silver tried in a furnace of earth, purified seven times. Ps. 12 : 6.

Wherewithal shall a young man cleanse his way? by taking heed thereto according to thy word. Thy word have I hid in mine heart, that I might not sin against thee. Ps. 119 : 9, 11.

Now ye are clean through the word which I have spoken unto you. John 15:3.

ENLIGHTENING.

The entrance of thy words giveth light; it giveth understanding to the simple Ps. 119: 130.

Thy word is a lamp unto my feet, and a light unto my path. Ps. 119 : 105.

The commandment is a lamp; and the law is a light. Prov. vi. 23. Thou, through thy commandments, hast made me wiser than mine enemies. I have more understanding than all my teachers; for thy testimonies are my meditation. I understand more than all the ancients, because I keep thy precepts. Ps. 119 : 98–100.

SURE.

Not one thing hath failed of all which the Lord your God spake concerning you; all are come to pass. Josh. 23 : 14.

Thy testimonies are very sure. Ps. 93:5.

The scripture cannot be broken. John 10 : 35.

The word of our God shall stand forever. Is. 40:8.

Heaven and earth shall pass away, but my word shall not pass away, Matt. 24:35.

TRUE.

Thy word is truth. John 17 : 17.

O send out thy light and thy truth.— Ps. 43 : 3.

Thy word is true from the beginning. Ps. 119 : 160. All thy commandments are truth. 151.

RIGHT.

The word of the Lord is right. Ps. 33:4.

I esteem all thy precepts concerning all things, to be right. Ps. 119 : 128.

The statutes of the Lord are right, rejoicing the heart. Ps. 19 : 8. They are all right to them that find knowledge. Prov. 8 : 9.

THE UNERRING STANDARD.

These were more noble than those in Thessalonica, in that they received the word with all readiness of mind, and searched the scriptures daily, whether these things were so Acts 15 : 11.

Give me understanding according to thy word. Ps. 119 : 169.

Ye do err not knowing the scriptures. Matt. 22:29. The wise men are ashamed ; they have rejected the word of the Lord ; and what wisdom is in them? Jer. 8 : 9. To the law and to the testimony: if they speak not according to this word, it is because there is no light in them. Is. 8 : 20.

LIFE-GIVING.

The law of the Lord is perfect, converting the soul. Ps. xix. 7.

Lord, to whom shall we go but unto thee? thou hast the words of eternal life. John vi. 68.

He that heareth my word, and believeth on him that sent me, hath everlasting life. John 5 : 24. Being born again, not of corruptible seed, but of incorruptible, by the word of God that liveth and abideth forever. 1 Pet. 1 : 23. Search the Scriptures; for in them ye think ye have eternal life; and they are they which testify of me. John 5:39.

PRECIOUS.

The word of the Lord was precious in those days. 1 Sam. 3 : 1.

How precious are thy thoughts unto me, O God! how great is the sum of them! Ps. 139 : 17.

I have rejoiced in the way of thy testimonies, as much as in all riches. 119 : 14.

The law of thy mouth is better unto me than thousands of gold or silver. 72.

I love thy commandments above gold; yea, above fine gold. 127.

I rejoice at thy word, as one that findeth great spoil. 162.

How sweet are thy words unto my taste! yea, sweeter than honey to my mouth! 103.

More to be desired are they than gold, yea, than much fine gold : sweeter also than honey and the honeycomb. 19:10.

Thy words were found, and I did eat them ; and thy word was unto me the joy and rejoicing of my heart. Jer. 15 : 16.

I have esteemed the words of his mouth more than my necessary food. Job 23 : 12.

As newborn babes, desire the sincere milk of the word, that ye may grow thereby. 1 Pet. 2 : 2. See Ps. 1 : 1-3 ; Jer. 20 : 8, 9.

PRACTICAL.

All scripture is given by inspiration of God, and is profitable for doctrine, for reproof, for correction, for instruction in righteousness, that the man of God may be perfect, throughly furnished unto all good works. 2 Tim. 3 : 16, 17.

The secret things belong unto the Lord our God : but those things which are revealed belong unto us and to our children for ever, that we may do all the words of this law. Deut. 29 : 29.

This book of the law shall not depart out of thy mouth ; but thou shalt meditate therein day and night, that thou mayest observe to do according to all that is written therein : for then thou shalt make thy way prosperous, and then thou shalt have good success. Josh. 1 : 8. See Matt. 7 : 14–27 ; Jas. 1 : 22–25.

Remember thy word unto thy servant upon which thou hast caused me to hope. Ps. 119 : 49.

These things have I written unto you that believe on the name of the Son of God ; that ye may know that ye have eternal life, and that ye may believe on the name of the Son of God. 1 John 5 : 13. See John 3 : 33 ; Rom. 15 : 4. Eph. 6 : 17 ; Heb. 4 : 12 ; Jer. 23 : 29.

PRAYER.

Ye have not, because ye ask not. Jas. 4 : 2. Ask, and ye shall receive. John 16 : 24.

O thou that hearest prayer, unto thee shall all flesh come. Ps. 65 : 2.

There is no difference between the Jew and the Greek; for the same Lord over all is rich unto all that call upon him. Rom. 10 : 12.

Hear, O, Lord, when I cry with my voice: have mercy also upon me and answer me. Ps. 27 : 7.

He will be very gracious unto thee at the voice of thy cry; when he shall hear it, he will answer thee. Is. 30 : 19.

Incline thine ear unto me; in the day when I call, answer me speedily. Ps. 102:2.

Before they call I will answer; and while they are yet speaking, I will hear. Is. 65 : 24.

My voice shalt thou hear in the morning, in the morning will I direct my prayer unto thee, and will look up. Ps. 5 : 3. Evening, and at morning, and at noon, will I pray, and cry aloud; and the Lord shall hear my voice. 55 : 17.

Pray without ceasing. 1 Thess. 5 : 17.

Men ought always to pray, and not to faint. Lu. 18 : 1.

STRENGTH.

In the day when I cried thou answeredst me, and strengthenedst me with strength in my soul. Ps. 108 : 3.

Give thy strength unto thy servant. Ps. 86 : 16.

As thy days, so shall thy strength be. Deut. 33 : 25.

Strengthen thou me according to thy word. Ps. 119 : 28.

He giveth power to the faint; and to them that have no might he increaseth strength. They that wait upon the Lord shall renew their strength. Is. 40 : 29, 31.

The people that do know their God shall be strong and do exploits. Dan. 11 : 32.

In quietness and in confidence shall be your strength. Is. 30 : 15.

When I am weak then am I strong. 2 Cor. 12 : 10.

My strength is made perfect in weakness. 2 Cor. 12 : 9.

I can do all things through Christ who strengtheneth me. Phil. 4 : 13.

Finally, my brethren, be strong in the Lord, and in the power of his might. Eph. 6 : 10. Strengthened with all might according to his glorious power. Col. 1 : 11.

GOD'S HOUSE.

And Jesus came to Nazareth, where he had been brought up; and, as his custom was, he went into the synagogue on the Sabbath day. Lu. 4: 16.

How amiable are thy tabernacles, O Lord of hosts! My soul longeth, yea, even fainteth for the courts of the Lord. Ps. 84: 1, 2.

Ye shall keep my Sabbaths, and reverence my sanctuary. Lev. 19: 30.

Blessed are they that dwell in thy house; they will be still praising thee. Ps. 84: 4.

In all places where I record my name I will come unto thee, and I will bless thee. Ex. 20: 24.

A day in thy courts is better than a thousand. I had rather be a doorkeeper in the house of my God, than to dwell in the tents of wickedness. Ps. 84: 10.

Where two or three are gathered together in my name, there am I in the the midst of them. Matt. 18: 20.

Not forsaking the assembling of ourselves together, as the manner of some is; but exhorting one another, and so much the more, as ye see the day approaching. Heb. 10: 25. See Ps. 73: 2, 3. John 20: 19–28.

TRUST IN GOD.

Bleseed is the man that maketh the Lord his trust. Ps. 40 : 4.

They that know thy name will put their trust in thee. Ps. 9:10.

That thy trust may be in the Lord, I have made known to thee this day, even to thee. Prov. 22:19.

In thee, O Lord, do I put my trust; let me never be put to confusion. Ps. 71:1.

Whoso putteth his trust in the Lord shall be safe. Prov. 29:25.

What time I am afraid, I will trust in thee. In God I have put my trust; I will not fear what flesh can do unto me. Ps. 56:3, 4.

Trust ye in the Lord for ever; for in the Lord Jehovah is everlasting strength. Is. 26:4.

The Lord is my rock, and my fortress, and the God of my rock; in him will I trust. 2 Sam. 22:2, 3.

They that trust in the Lord shall be as Mount Zion, which cannot be removed, but abideth for ever. Ps. 125:1.

Behold, God is my salvation; I will trust, and not be afraid; for the Lord Jehovah is my strength and my song; he also is become my salvation. Is. 12:2.

TO BE KEPT.

Kept by the power of God. 1 Pet. 1:5

O that thou wouldest bless me indeed, and that thou wouldest keep me from evil 1 Chron. 4:10.

The Lord bless thee and keep thee. Num. 6:24. The Lord shall preserve thee from all evil. Ps. 121:7.

Be thou my strong habitation, whereunto I may continually resort; for thou art my rock and my fortress. Ps. 71:1, 3.

Because thou hast made the Lord, which is my refuge, even the most High, thy habitation; there shall no evil befall thee. Ps. 91:9, 10.

He that dwelleth in the secret place of the most High shall abide under the shadow of the Almighty. Ps. 91:1.

He shall dwell on high: his place of defence shall be the munitions of rocks; bread shall be given him; his waters shall be sure. Is. 33:16.

Thou shalt hide them in the secret of thy presence from the pride of man; thou shalt keep them secretly in a pavilion from the strife of tongues. Ps. 27:5.

The eternal God is thy refuge; and underneath are the everlasting arms. Deut. 33:27.

TO BE KEPT.

The Lord is thy keeper. Ps. 121 : 5.

Keep me as the apple of the eye. Ps. 17 : 8.

He that toucheth you toucheth the apple of his eye. Zech. 2 : 8.

Hide me under the shadow of thy wings. Ps. 17 : 8.

He shall cover thee with his feathers, and under his wings shalt thou trust. Ps. 91 : 4.

How excellent is thy loving-kindness, O God! therefore the children of men put their trust under the shadow of thy wings. Ps. 36 : 7.

And Boaz said unto Ruth, the Lord recompense thy work, and a full reward be given thee of the Lord God of Israel, under whose wings thou art come to trust. Ruth 2 : 11, 12.

Because thou hast been my help, therefore in the shadow of thy wings will I rejoice. Ps. 63 : 7. I will trust in the covert of thy wings. 61 : 4.

Now unto him that is able to keep you from falling, and to present you faultless before the presence of his glory with exceeding joy, to the only wise God our Saviour, be glory and majesty, dominion and power, both now and ever. Ju. 24, 25.

A MEDIATOR.

He saw that there was no man, and wondered that there was no intercessor. Is. 59 : 16.

If one man sin against another, the judge shall judge him; but if a man sin against the Lord, who shall entreat for him? 1 Sam. 2 : 25. For he is not a man, as I am, that we should come together in judgment. Neither is there any daysman betwixt us, that might lay his hand upon us both. Job 9 : 32, 33.

There is one God, and one Mediator between God and man, the man Christ Jesus. 1 Tim. 2 : 5.

O that one might plead for a man with God, as a man pleadeth for his neighbor! Job 16 : 21.

I have prayed for thee, that thy faith fail not. Lu. 22 : 31, 32.

If any man sin, we have an advocate with the Father, Jesus Christ the righteous. 1 John 2 : 1. Who is even at the right hand of God, who also maketh intercession for us. Rom. 8 : 34.

I pray not for the world, but for them whom thou hast given me. Neither for these only do I pray, but for them also that believe on me through their word. John 17 : 9, 20.

SALVATION.

By grace are ye saved through faith. Eph. 2 : 8.

What must I do to be saved? Acts 16 : 30.

Believe on the Lord Jesus Christ, and thou shalt be saved. Acts 16 : 31. For God so loved the world, that he gave his only begotten Son, that whosoever believeth in him should not perish, but have everlasting life. John 3 : 16.

O Lord, save me, and I shall be saved. Jer. 17 : 14.

Whosoever shall call upon the name of the Lord shall be saved. Rom. 10 : 13.

I will cry unto God. He shall send from heaven and save me. Ps. 57 : 2, 3.

Say not in thine heart, who shall ascend into heaven? (to bring Christ down from above.) Or, descend into the deep? (to bring up Christ from the dead.) The word is nigh thee, even in thy mouth, and in thy heart, the word of faith, which we preach; that if thou shalt confess with thy mouth the Lord Jesus, and shalt believe in thine heart that God hath raised him from the dead, thou shalt be saved. For with the heart man believeth unto righteousness; and with the mouth confession is made unto salvation. Rom. 9 : 6–10.

MUTUAL LOVE AND LONGINGS.

I am my Beloved's, and his desire is toward me. Cant. 7:10.

The Lord is my portion, saith my soul. Lam. 3 : 24.

The Lord's portion is his people. Deut. 32 : 9.

Lord, thou knowest that I love thee. John 21 : 15.

I have loved thee with an everlasting love, therefore with loving-kindness have I drawn thee. Jer. 31 : 3.

Whom have I in heaven but thee: and there is none upon earth that I desire beside thee. Ps. 73 : 25.

Since thou wast precious in my sight, thou hast been honorable, and I have loved thee; therefore will I give men for thee, and people for thy life. Is. 43:4.

Set me as a seal upon thine heart, as a seal upon thine arm; for love is strong as death; jealousy is cruel as the grave. Cant. 8:6.

Behold I have graven thee upon the palms of my hands. Is. 49:16. Thou shalt also be a crown of glory in the hand of the Lord, and a royal diadem in the hand of thy God. 62:3. And they shall be mine, saith the Lord, in that day when I make up my jewels. Mal. 3:17

HELP IN TROUBLE.

The Lord will be a refuge for the oppressed, a refuge in times of trouble. Ps. 9 : 9.

Be not far from me, for trouble is near. Ps. 22 : 11.

When he giveth quietness, who then can make trouble. Job 34 : 29.

Give us help from trouble: for vain is the help of man. Ps. 6 : 11.

Call upon me in the day of trouble; I will deliver thee, and thou shalt glorify me. Ps. 50 : 15.

The troubles of my heart are enlarged; O bring thou me out of my distresses. Ps. 25 : 17.

He shall deliver thee in six troubles; yea, in seven there shall no evil touch thee. Job 5 : 19.

O Lord, for thy name's sake; for thy righteousness'. sake, bring my soul out of trouble. Ps. 143 : 11.

Thou calledst in trouble, and I delivered thee.' Ps. 81 : 7.

God is our refuge and strength, a very present help in trouble. Ps. 46 : 1. For in the time of trouble he shall hide me in his pavilion; in the secret of his tabernacle shall he hide me; he shall set me up upon a rock. Ps. 27 : 5.

COMFORT FOR THE AFFLICTED.

The more they afflicted them, the more they multiplied and grew. Ex. 1 : 12.

Wherefore doth a living man complain, a man for the punishment of his sins? Lam. 3 : 29.

You only have I known of all the families of the earth; therefore I will punish you for all your iniquities.

Blessed is the man whom thou chastenest, O, Lord, and teachest him out of thy law. Ps. 94 : 12.

As many as I love, I rebuke and chasten; be zealous therefore and repent. Rev. 3 : 19. My son, despise not the chastening of the Lord; neither be weary of his correction; for whom the Lord loveth he correcteth; even as a father the son in whom he delighteth. Prov. 3 : 11, 12.

It is good for me that I have been afflicted. Ps. 119 : 71. Before I was afflicted I went astray; but now have I kept thy word. 67. See Heb. 12 : 11.

Beloved, think it not strange concerning the fiery trial which is to try you, as though some strange thing happened unto you. But rejoice, inasmuch as ye are partakers of Christ's sufferings; that, when his glory shall be revealed, ye may be glad also with exceeding joy. 1 Pet. 4 : 12, 13.

Comfort.

Light is sown for the righteous and gladness for the upright in heart. Ps. 97 : 11.

Whatsoever things were written aforetime were written for our learning, that we through patience and comfort of the scriptures might have hope. Rom. 15 : 4.

The Comforter, which is the Holy Ghost, whom the Father will send in my name, he shall teach you all things, and bring all things to your remembrance, whatsoever I have said unto you John 14 : 26.

In the multitude of my thoughts within me thy comforts delight my soul. Ps. 94 : 19.

Now, our Lord Jesus Christ himself, and God, even our Father, which hath loved us, and hath given us everlasting consolation and good hope through grace, comfort your hearts. 2 Thess. 2 : 16.

Blessed be God, even the father of our Lord Jesus Christ, the father of mercies, and the God of all comfort ; who comforteth us in all our tribulation, that we may be able to comfort them which are in any trouble, by the comfort wherewith we ourselves are comforted of God. 2 Cor. 1 : 3, 4.

COMFORT IN SORROW.

Then had the churches rest and were edified; and walking in the fear of the Lord, and in the comfort of the Holy Ghost, were multiplied. Acts 9 : 31.

O that I could comfort myself against sorrow. Jer. 8 : 18.

Comfort ye, comfort ye my people, saith your God. Is. 40 : 1.

I sigh; and there is none to comfort me. Lam. 1 : 21.

I, even I, am he that comforteth you. Is. 51 : 12.

I looked for comforters, but I found none. Ps. 69 : 20.

As one whom his mother comforteth, so will I comfort you. Is. 66 : 13.

Mine eyes fail for thy word, when wilt thou comfort me? Ps. 110 : 82.

I will not leave you comfortless; I will come to you. John 14 : 18.

I weep; mine eye runneth down with water, because the comforter that should relieve my soul is far from me. Lam. 1:16.

I will pray the father, and he shall give you another Comforter, that he may abide with you forever. John 14 : 16.

COMFORT TO MOURNERS.

God that comforteth those that are cast down. 2 Cor. 7 : 6.

Mine eye mourneth by reason of affliction. Ps. 88 : 9.
Blessed are they that mourn ; for they shall be comforted. Matt. 5 : 4.

Why go I mourning because of the oppression of the enemy? Ps. 42 : 9. I am bowed down greatly ; I go mourning all the day long. 38 : 6.

I will restore comforts unto mourners. Is. 57 : 18. I will turn their mourning into joy, and will comfort them, and make them rejoice from their sorrow. Jer. 31 : 13

Thou hast turned for me my mourning into dancing ; thou hast put off my sackcloth, and girded me with gladness. Ps. 30 : 11.

The Lord has sent me to bind up the broken hearted, to comfort all that mourn, to give unto them beauty for ashes, the oil of joy for mourning, the garment of praise for the spirit of heaviness. Is. 61 : 1–3.

JOY.

Finally, my brethren, rejoice in the Lord. Phil. 3 : 1.

Then Philip went down to the city of Samaria, and preached Christ unto them. And there was great joy in that city. Acts 8 : 5, 8.

Behold, I bring you good tidings of great joy, which shall be to all people. For unto you is born this day in the city of David a Saviour, which is Christ the Lord. Lu. 2 : 10, 11.

Blessed is the people that know the joyful sound; they shall walk, O, Lord, in the light of thy countenance. In thy name shall they rejoice all the day. Ps. 89 : 15, 16.

These things have I spoken unto you, that my joy might remain in you, and that your joy might be full. John 15 : 11.

We joy in God through our Lord Jesus Christ, by whom we have now received the atonement. Rom. 5 : 11.

Whom having not seen, ye love; in whom, thou now ye see him not, yet believing, ye rejoice with joy unspeakable and full of glory. 1 Peter 1 : 8.

JOY.

Rejoice in the Lord alway; and again I say, rejoice. Phil. 4 : 3.

Wilt thou not revive us again; that thy people may rejoice in thee? Ps. 85 : 3.

Ask, and ye shall receive, that your joy may be full. John 16 : 24.

Restore unto me the joy of thy salvation; and uphold me with thy free spirit. Then will I teach transgressors thy ways. and sinners shall be converted unto thee; Ps. 51 : 12, 13.

Rejoice not that the spirits are subject unto you; but rejoice because your names are written in heaven. Lu. 10 : 20.

My soul shall be joyful in the Lord; it shall rejoice in his salvation. Ps. 33 : 9.

With joy shall ye draw water out of the wells of salvation. Is. 12 : 3.

Thou meetest him that rejoiceth and worketh righteousness, those that remember thee in thy ways. Is. 64 : 5.

Go your way, eat the fat, and drink the sweet, and send portions unto them for whom nothing is prepared; neither be ye sorry; for the joy of the Lord is your strength. Neh. 8 : 10.

JOY.

The voice of rejoicing and salvation is in the tabernacles of the righteous. Ps. 118 : 5.

We will rejoice in thy salvation, and in the name of our God we will set up our banners. Ps. 20 : 5.

Be glad in the Lord, and rejoice, ye righteous; and shout for joy, and ye that are upright in heart. Ps. 35 : 9.

My lips shall greatly rejoice when I sing unto thee; and my soul, which thou hast redeemed. Ps. 71 : 23.

Let the righteous be glad; let them rejoice before God: yea, let them exceedingly rejoice. Ps. 68 : 3.

I will greatly rejoice in the Lord, my soul shall be joyful in my God; for he hath clothed me with the garments of salvation, he hath covered me with the robe of righteousness, as a bridegroom decketh himself with ornaments, and as a bride adorneth herself with her jewels. Is 61:10.

Let the saints be joyful in glory; let them sing aloud upon their beds. Ps. 149:5 Let all those that put their trust in thee rejoice; let them ever shout for joy, because thou defendest them; let them also that love thy name be joyful in thee. 5 : 11.

JOY IN SORROW.

As sorrowful yet always rejoicing. 2 Cor. 6:10.

Blessed are they which are persecuted for righteousness' sake; for their's is the kingdom of heaven. Matt. 6:10.

Blessed are ye, when men shall revile you, and persecute you, and shall say all manner of evil against you falsely, for my sake. Rejoice, and be exceeding glad; for great is your reward in heaven; for so persecuted they the prophets which were before you. Matt. 6:11, 12.

Thou hast put gladness in my heart, more than in the time that their corn and their wine increased. Ps. 4:7.

The poor among men shall rejoice in the Holy One of Israel. Is. 29:19.

Although the fig tree shall not blossom, neither shall fruit be in the vines; the labor of the olive shall fail, and the fields shall yield no meat; the flock shall be cut off from the fold, and there shall be no herd in the stalls: Yet I will rejoice in the Lord, I will joy in the God of my salvation. Neh. 8:10.

REJOICING IN HOPE.

Rejoice evermore. 1 Thess. 5 : 16.

Weeping may endure for a night, but joy cometh in the morning. Ps. 30 : 5.

Blessed are ye that weep now, for ye shall laugh. Lu. 6 : 21.

They that sow in tears shall reap in joy ; he that goeth forth and weepeth, bearing precious seed shall doubtless come again with rejoicing, bringing his sheaves with him. Ps. 126 : 5, 6.

Ye shall weep and lament, but your sorrow shall be turned into joy, and your joy no man taketh from you. John 16 : 20, 22.

The ransomed of the Lord shall come to Zion with songs and everlasting joy upon their heads ; they shall obtain joy and gladness, and sorrow and sighing shall flee away. Is. 35 : 10.

They shall hunger no more, neither thirst any more ; neither shall the sun light on them, nor any heat. For the Lamb which is in the midst of the throne shall feed them, and shall lead them unto living fountains of waters ; and God shall wipe away all tears from their eyes. Rev. 7 : 16, 17.

PRAYER.

"*Behold he prayeth.*" Acts 9 : 11.

Hearken unto the voice of my cry, my King, and my God: for unto thee will I pray. Ps. 5 : 2.

Thus saith the Lord, the Holy One of Israel, and his Maker, Ask me of things to come concerning my sons, and concerning the work of my hands command ye me. Is. 45 : 11.

Let my prayer be set forth before thee as incense; and the lifting up of my hands as the evening sacrifice. Ps. 141 : 2.

The eyes of the Lord are upon the righteous, and his ears are open unto their cry. Ps. 34 : 15. The prayer of the upright is his delight. Prov. 15 : 8.

And the four beasts and four and twenty elders fell down before the Lamb, having every one of them harps, and golden vials full of odours, which are the prayers of saints. Rev. 5 : 8.

And another angel came and stood at the altar, having a golden censer; and there was given unto him much incense, that he should offer it with the prayers of all saints upon the golden altar which was before the throne. And the smoke of the incense, which came with the prayers of the saints, ascended up before God out of the angel's hand. 8 : 3, 4.

CONDITIONS OF PREVAILING PRAYER.

Lord teach us to pray. Lu. 11 : 1.

CHARACTER AND CONDUCT.

Delight thyself also in the Lord; and he shall give thee the desires of thine heart. Ps. 37 : 4. The desire of the righteous shall be granted. Prov. 10 : 4. See Ps. 34 : 15-17; 145 : 19; John 9 : 31; 1 John 3 : 21, 22.

SONSHIP.

When ye pray, say Our Father who art in heaven. Lu. 11 : 2. For if ye, being evil, know how to give good gifts unto your children: how much more shall your heavenly Father give the Holy Spirit, (good things. Matt. 7 : 11), to them that ask him? 13.

FAITH.

All things whatsoever ye shall ask in prayer, believing, ye shall receive. Matt. 21 : 22. See 1 Chron. 5 : 18-20; 2 Chron. 14 : 11, 12. Mark : 11 24.

OBEDIENCE.

Now we know that God heareth not sinners; but if any man be a worshipper of God, and doeth his will, him he heareth. John 9 : 31. If ye abide in me, and my words abide in you, ye shall ask what ye will, and it shall be done unto you. 15:7

CONDITIONS OF PREVAILING PRAYER.

Quicken us, and we will call upon thy name. Ps. 80 : 12.

THE HOLY SPIRIT.

Praying always with all prayer and supplication in the spirit. Eph. 6 : 18. Praying in the Holy Ghost. Jude 20. See Zech. 12 : 10 ; Rom. 8 : 16, 27.

THE NAME OF CHRIST.

No man cometh unto the Father but by me. John 14 : 6. If ye shall ask anything in my name, I will do it. 14. See 16 : 23. Eph 2 : 18.

AGREEMENT WITH GOD'S WILL.

If we ask anything according to his will he heareth us. 1 John 5 : 14. See Ps. 37 : 4 ; John 15 : 7.

HUMILITY.

Lord, thou hast heard the desire of the humble ; thou wilt prepare their heart, thou wilt cause their ear to hear. Ps. 10 : 17. See 2 Chron. 7 : 14 ; 33 : 12, 13 ; 34 : 26, 27.

THANKFULNESS.

Be careful for nothing ; but in everything by prayer and supplication, with thanksgiving, let your requests be made known unto God. Phil. 4 : 6, 7.

CONDITIONS OF PREVAILING PRAYER.

The Lord fulfil all thy petitions. Ps. 20 : 5.

REVERENCE.

Be not rash with thy mouth, and let not thine heart be hasty to utter anything before God; for God is in heaven and thou upon earth; therefore let thy words be few. Ecc. 5 : 3. Ps. 95 : 6. Rev. 4 : 8-11 ; 5 : 8 14 ; 7 : 11.

SIMPLICITY.

When ye pray, use not vain repetitions as the heathen do; for they think that they shall be heard for their much speaking. Matt. 6 : 7. See 1 Kings 18 : 26-28 ; 36 : 37 ; 1 Chron. 4 : 10.

SINCERITY.

The Lord is nigh unto all that call upon him in truth. Ps. 145 : 18. See 17 : 1. John 11 : 23, 24.

EARNESTNESS AND PERSISTENCY.

There is none that calleth upon thy name, that stirreth up himself to take hold of thee. Is. 64 : 7. The effectual fervent prayer of a righteous man availeth much. Jas. 5 : 16. See Gen. 32 : 24, 29 ; Lu. 11 : 5-8 ; 18 : 1-8 ; 6 : 12 ; Matt. 26 : 36-44 : Heb. 5 : 7.

LOVE.

Now abideth faith, hope, love, these three; but the greatest of these is love. 1 Cor. 13 : 13.

I will love thee, O Lord, my strength. Ps. 18 : 1.

Thou shalt love the Lord thy God with all thy heart, and with all thy soul, and with all thy mind, and with all thy strength; this is the first commandment. Mark 12 : 30.

Lord, thou knowest that I love thee. John 21 : 15.

I have loved thee with an everlasting love, therefore with loving-kindness have I drawn thee. Jer. 31 : 3.

Herein is love, not that we loved God, but that he loved us, and sent his Son to be the propitiation for our sins. We love him, because he first loved us. 1 John 4 : 10, 19.

As the Father hath loved me, so I loved you; continue ye in my love. John 16 : 9.

BROTHERLY LOVE.

Behold how good and how pleasant it is for brethren to dwell together in unity. Ps. 133 : 1. Love suffereth long, and is kind; is not easily provoked; thinketh no evil; beareth all things, hopeth all things, believeth all things. 1 Cor. 13 : 4-7.

Beloved let us love one another; for love is of God; and every one that loveth is begotten of God, and knoweth God. He that loveth not knoweth not God, for God is love. In this was manifested the love of God toward us, because that God sent his only begotten Son into the world that we might live through him. If God so loved us, we ought also to love one another. 1 John 4 : 7-11.

A new commandment I give unto you, that ye love one another; as I have loved you, that ye also love one another. By this shall all men know that ye are my disciples, if ye have love to one another. John 13 : 34, 35.

We know that we have passed from death unto life because we love the brethren. 1 John 3 : 14.

Let brotherly love continue. Heb. 13:1
See Col. 2 : 2 ; 1 Pet. 1 : 22 ; 3 : 8.

OBEDIENCE.

To obey is better than sacrifice, and to hearken than the fat of rams. 1 Sam. 15 : 22.

I will run the way of thy commandments, when thou shalt enlarge my heart. Ps. 119 : 32.

O that thou hadst hearkened to my commandments! then had thy peace been as a river, and thy righteousness as the waves of the sea. Is. 48 : 18, 1 : 19.

Make me to go in the path of thy commandments; for therein do I delight. Ps. 119 : 35.

I will put my Spirit within you, and cause you to walk in my statutes, and do them. Ez. 36 : 27.

My soul hath kept thy testimonies; and I love them exceedingly. Ps. 119 : 167.

If any man will do his will, he shall know of the doctrine. John 7 : 17; 13 : 17.

Not every one that saith unto me, Lord, Lord, shall enter into the kingdom of heaven; but he that doeth the will of my Father which is in heaven. Matt. 7 : 21. See vers. 24-27. Jas. 1 : 22-25. Ecc. 12:13.

OBEDIENCE.

Though he were a Son, yet learned he obedience by the things which he suffered; and being made perfect, he became the author of eternal salvation unto all them that obey him. Heb. 5 : 9.

This is the love of God, that we keep his commandments. 1 John, 5 : 3.

If ye love me, ye will keep my commandments. John 14 : 15.

He that keepeth his commandments dwelleth in him, and he in him. John 3 : 14.

If a man love me, he will keep my words; and my Father will love him, and we will come unto him, and make our abode with him. John 14 : 23

Hereby do we know that we know him, if we keep his commandments Whoso keepeth his word, in him verily is the love of God perfected. 1 John 2 : 3, 5.

If ye keep my commandments, ye shall abide in my love; even as I have kept my Father's commandments, and abide in his love. John 15 : 10.

Ye are my friends, if ye do whatsoever I command you. John 15 : 14.

LIGHT.

Unto the upright there ariseth light in the darkness. Ps. 112 : 4.

O send out thy light and thy truth; let them lead me. Ps. 43 : 3. In thy light shall we see light. 36:9.

Arise, shine; for thy light is come, the glory of the Lord is risen upon th. Is. 60 : 1. See Eph. 5 : 14.

The Lord is my light and my salvation. Ps. 27 : 1. The Lord my God will enlighten my darkness. 18 : 28.

I am come a light into the world, that whosoever believeth on me should not abide in darkness. John 12 : 46.

The Lord will bring me forth to the light; when I sit in darkness, the Lord shalt be a light unto me. Mic. 7 : 8, 9.

I am the light of the world; he that followeth me shall not walk in darkness, but shall have the light of life. John 8:12.

O come, and let us walk in the light of the Lord. Is. 2 : 5. If we walk in the light, as he is in the light, we have fellowship one with another, and the blood of Jesus Christ his Son cleanseth us from all sin. 1 John 1 : 7.

Ye are the children of light, and the children of the day. 1 Thess. 5 : 5.

Walk as children of light. Eph. 5 : 8. See Matt. 5 : 14, 16; 2 Cor. 4 : 6; Phil. 2 : 14, 15; 1 Pet. 2 : 4.

PROVIDED FOR

The Lord will give grace and glory ; no good thing will he withhold from them that walk uprightly. Ps. 84 : 11.

The Lord is my shepherd ; I shall not want. Ps. 23 : 1.

Fear the Lord, ye his saints ; for there is no want to them that fear him. They that seek the Lord shall not want any good thing. Ps. 34 : 9, 10.

The eyes of all wait upon thee ; and thou givest them their meat in due season. Thou openest thine hand and satisfiest the desire of every living thing. Ps. 145 : 15, 16.

Take no thought for your life, what ye shall eat, or what ye shall drink ; nor yet for your body, what ye shall put on. Behold the fowls of the air : for they sow not, neither do they reap, nor gather into barns ; yet your heavenly Father feedeth them. Are ye not much better than they ? Matt. 6 : 25, 26.

He that spared not his own Son, but delivered him up for us all, how shall he not with him also freely give us all things ? Rom. 8 : 32.

My God shall supply all your need according to his riches in glory by Christ Jesus. Eph. 4 : 19.

FILLED.

It pleased the Father that in him should all fulness dwell. Col. 1: 19. See 2 : 9.

He filleth the hungry with goodness. Ps. 107 : 9.

Blessed are they which do hunger and thirst after righteousness, for they shall be filled. Matt. 5 : 6. Open thy mouth wide, and I will fill it. Ps. 81 : 10.

The disciples were filled with joy, and with the Holy Ghost. Acts 13 : 52.

Now the God of hope fill you with all joy and peace in believing, that ye may abound in hope, through the power of the Holy Ghost. Rom. 15 : 13.

I am full of power by the spirit of the Lord. Mic. 3 : 8.

Be filled with the Spirit. Eph. 5 : 18.

For this cause I bow my knees unto Father of our Lord Jesus Christ, that he would grant you, according to the riches of his glory, to be strengthened with might by his Spirit in the inner man, that Christ may dwell in your hearts by faith ; That ye may be able to comprehend with all saints what is the breadth, and length, and depth, and height ; and to know the love of Christ, which passeth knowledge, that ye might be filled with all the fulness of God. Eph. 3 : 14-19.

SATISFIED.

O Naphtali, satisfied with favor. Deut. 33 : 23. See Ps. 107 : 9. 145 : 16.

O satisfy us early with thy mercy, that we may rejoice and be glad all our days. Ps. 90 : 14.

Wherefore do ye spend money for that which is not bread? and your labor for that which satisfieth not? hearken diligently unto me, and eat ye that which is good, and let your soul delight itself in fatness. Is. 55 : 2.

My soul shall be satisfied as with marrow and fatness, and my mouth shall praise thee with joyful lips. Ps. 63 : 5.

I will satiate the soul of the priests with fatness, and my people shall be satisfied with my goodness, saith the Lord. Jer. 31 : 14.

They shall be abundantly satisfied with the fatness of thy house; and thou shalt make them drink of the river of thy pleasures. Ps. 36 : 8.

The Lord upholdeth the righteous, and in the days of famine they shall be satisfied. Ps. 37 : 17, 19.

We shall be satisfied with the goodness of thy house, even of thy holy temple. 65 : 4. As for me, I will behold thy face in righteousness; I shall be satisfied when I awake with thy likeness. 17 : 15.

SANCTIFIED.

The Lord hath set apart him that is godly for himself, Ps. 4 : 3 ; sanctified by God the Father, Jude 1 ; in Christ Jesus, 1 Cor. 1:2 ; by the Spirit of God, 1 Cor. 6 : 11 ; through the truth, John 17 : 17, 19.

Christ loved the church, and gave himself for it ; that he might sanctify and cleanse it with the washing of water by the word. Eph. 5 : 25, 26.

This is the will of God, even your sanctification. 1 Thess. 4 : 3.

By which will we have been sanctified through the offering of the body of Jesus Christ once for all. For by one offering he hath perfected for ever them that are sanctified. Heb. 10 : 10, 14.

Sanctify yourselves therefore for I am the Lord which sanctify you. Lu. 20 : 7,8.

In a great house there are not only vessels of gold and of silver, but also of wood and of earth ; and some to honor, and some to dishonor. If a man therefore purge himself from these, he shall be a vessel unto honor, sanctified, and meet for the master's use, and prepared unto every good work. 2 Tim. 2 : 20, 21.

Abstain from all appearance of evil. And the very God of peace sanctify you wholly. 1 Thess. 5 : 22, 23. See 2 Cor.

HOLINESS.

An highway shall be there, and it shall be called the way of holiness. Is. 35 : 8. *And they shall call them the holy people, the redeemed of the Lord* 62 : 12.

God hath called us unto holiness. 1 Thess. 4 : 7.

As he which hath called you is holy, so be ye holy in all manner of conversation; because it is written, be ye holy; for I am holy. 1 Pet. 1 : 15, 16.

Blessed be the God and Father of our Lord Jesus Christ, who hath chosen us in him before the foundation of the world, that we should be holy and without blame before him in love Eph. 1 : 3, 4.

Ye, also, as lively stones, are built up a spiritual house, an holy priesthood, to offer up spiritual sacrifices, acceptable to God by Jesus Christ. 1 Pet. 2 : 5.

Holiness becometh thine house, O Lord, for ever. Ps. 93 : 5.

Know ye not that ye are the temple of God, and that the Spirit of God dwelleth in you? If any man defile the temple of God, him shall God destroy; for the temple of God is holy, which temple ye are. 1 Cor. 3 : 16, 17.

See 2 Cor. 7 : 1; Rom. 12 : 1; Heb. 12 : 14.

CHRIST'S SECOND COMING.

Looking for that blessed hope, and the glorious appearing of the great God and our Saviour Jesus Christ. Tit. 2 : 13.

Behold, he cometh with clouds, and every eye shall see him. Rev. 1 : 7.

Ye shall see the Son of Man coming in the clouds of heaven. Matt. 26 : 64.

The Lord my God shall come, and all the saints with thee. Zech. 14 : 5.

Behold the Lord cometh with ten thousand of his saints. Jude 14.

Our God shall come, and shall not keep silence. Ps. 50 : 3.

The Lord himself shall descend from heaven with a shout, with the voice of the archangel, and with the trump of God, and the dead in Christ shall rise first. 1 Thess. 4 : 16.

Then we which are alive and remain, shall be caught up together with them in the clouds to meet the Lord in the air; and so shall we ever be with the Lord. 1 Thess. 4 : 17.

I go to prepare a place for you And if I go and prepare a place for you, I will come again and receive you unto myself; that where I am, there ye may be also John 14 : 3.

CHRIST'S SECOND COMING.

Looking for and hasting the coming of the day of God. 2 Pet. 3 : 12. Waiting for the coming of our Lord Jesus Christ. 1 Cor. 1 : 7.

Our conversation is in heaven; from whence also we look for the Saviour, the Lord Jesus Christ. Phil. 3 : 20.

This same Jesus, which is taken up from you into heaven, shall so come in like manner as ye have seen him go into heaven. Acts 1 : 71. And unto them that look for him he shall appear the second time without sin unto salvation. Heb. 9 : 28.

There is laid up for me a crown of righteousness, which the Lord, the righteous judge, shall give me at that day; and not to me only, but unto all them also that love his appearing. 2 Tim. 4 : 8.

The Lord direct your hearts into the love of God, and into the patient waiting for Christ. 2 Thess. 3 : 5.

A very little while and he that cometh shall come and shall not tarry. Heb. 10 : 37.

Behold, I come quick quickly; and my reward is with me, to give every man according as his work shall be. Rev. 22 : 12. See 22 : 20. 1 : 7.

GOD'S PRESENCE.

The Lord was with Joseph, and he was a prosperous man. Gen. 39 : 2.

"If God will be with me, and keep me in this way that I go, and give me bread to eat, and raiment to put on, so that I come again to my father's house in peace, then shall the Lord be my God. Gen. 28 : 20-22.

"Behold, I am with thee, and will keep thee in all places whither thou goest, and will bring thee again into this land ; for I will not leave thee until I have done that which I have spoken to thee of." Gen. 28 : 15.

"If thy presence go not with me, carry us not hence." Ex. 33 : 15.

"Certainly I will be with thee." Ex. 3 : 12. "My presence shall go with thee, and I will give the rest." 33 : 14. See Josh. 1 : 9.

"Though I walk through the valley of the shadow of death, I will fear no evil, for thou art with me." Ps. 23 : 4. See Num. 14 : 9 ; 2 Chron. 32 : 7, 8 ; Ps. 46 : 1-7 ; Is. 8 : 9, 10.

Fear not, for I am with thee." Is. xii:2-5. See Gen. 45 3, 4 ; Deut. 20 : 1-4 ; 31 : 6-8; Judges 6 : 16 ; 1 Sam. 10 : 7 ; 1 Chron. 17 : 2 ; 2 Chron. 20 : 17 ; Jer. 1 : 8 ; Hag. 2 : 4; Matt. 18 : 19, 20 ; Acts 18 : 9, 10.

GOD SEES.

The eyes of the Lord are in every place, beholding the evil and the good. Prof. 15 ; 3. His eyes are upon the ways of man, aud he seeth all his goings. Job. 34 : 21. He knoweth the secrets of the heart. Ps. 44 ; 21.

Thou God seest me. Gen. 16 : 13.

Can any hide himself in secret places that I shall not see him? Do not I fill heaven and earth? saith the Lord. Jer. 23 : 24.

Search me, O God, and know my heart; try me, and know my thoughts. Ps. 139 : 23. For thou, even thou only, knowest the hearts of all the children of men. 1 Kings 8 : 39.

I am he which searcheth the reins and hearts. Rev. 2 : 23.

O Lord, thou hast searched me, and known me. Thou knowest my downsitting and mine uprising ; thou understandest my thoughts afar off. For there is not a word in my tongue, but lo, O God, thou knowest it altogether. Ps. 139 : 1, 2, 4. For the Lord searcheth all hearts and understandeth all the imaginations of the thoughts. 1 Chron. 28 : 9.

I, the Lord, search the heart, I try the reins to give to every man according to

BACKSLIDING.

The backslider in heart shall be filled with his own ways. Prov. 14 : 14.

O Lord, our backslidings are many : we have sinned against thee. Jer. 14 : 7

My people are bent to backsliding from me. Hos. 11 : 7. They are gone away backward. Is. 1 : 4. My people have committed two evils ; they have forsaken me the fountain of living waters, and hewed them out cisterns, broken cisterns that can hold no water. Jer. 2 : 13.

Peter went out and wept bitterly. Matt. 26 : 75.

Thine own wickedness shall correct thee, and thy backslidings shall reprove thee ; know therefore and see that it is an evil thing and bitter, that thou hast forsaken the Lord thy God. Jer. 2 : 19.

And when he had spent all, there arose a mighty famine in that land ; and he began to be in want. Lu. 15 : 14.

Cursed be the man that trusteth in man, and maketh flesh his arm, and whose heart departeth from the Lord. For he shall be like the heath in the desert, and shall not see when good cometh : but shall inhabit the parched places in the wilderness, in a salt land and not inhabited. Jer. 17 : 5, 6.

RETURNING.

And when he came to himself he said, I will arise and go unto my father. Luke 15 : 17, 18. See Matt. 16 : 75.

Turn thou us unto thee, O, Lord. and we shall be turned ; renew our days as of old. Lam. 5 : 21.

O Israel, thou hast destroyed thyself ; but in me is thine help. Hos. 13 : 9.

Turn thou me, and I shall be turned ; for thou art the Lord my God. Jer. 31:18.

Return unto me, and I will return unto you, saith the Lord of Hosts. Mal. 3 : 7.

Let us search and try our ways, and turn again to the Lord. Lam. 3 : 40.

Return, ye backsliding children, and I will heal your backslidings. Jer. 3 : 22.

Come, and let us return unto the Lord; for he hath torn, and he will heal us; he hath smitten, and he will bind us up. Hos. 6 : 1.

Return unto me : for I have redeemed thee. Is. 44 : 22.

Behold, we come unto thee ; for thou art the Lord our God. Jer. 3 : 22.

Turn, O backsliding children, saith the Lord ; for I am married unto you. Jer. 3 : 14. See Hos. 14 : 1-4 ; Lu. 15 : 11-24; Rev. 2 : 4, 5 ; 3 : 15-20.

UPHELD.

Ths Lord upholdeth the righteous. Ps. 37 : 17.

Uphold me according unto thy word. Hold thou me up and I shall be safe. Ps. 119 : 116, 117. My soul followeth hard after thee ; thy right hand upholdeth me. 63 : 8.

Fear thou not ; for I am with thee ; be not dismayed ; for I am thy God ; I will strengenth thee, yea, I will help thee ; yea, I will uphold thee with the right hand of my righteousness. I the Lord thy God will hold thy right hand. Is. 41 : 10, 13.

Hold up my goings in thy paths that my footsteps slip not, (be not moved.) Ps. 17 : 5.

He will keep the feet of his saints. 1 Sam. 2 : 9. He will not suffer thy foot to be moved. Ps. 121 : 3.

Rejoice not against me, O man's enemy; when I fall I shall arise Mic. 7 : 8. When I said, my foot slippeth ; thy mercy, O Lord, held me up. Ps. 94 : 13.

The steps of a good man are ordered of the Lord ; and he delighteth in his ways. Though he fall, he shall not be utterly cast down : for the Lord upholdeth him with his hand. None of his steps shall slide. Ps. 37 : 23, 24, 31. Yea he shall be holden up ; for God is able to make him stand. Rom. 14 : 4.

NOT FORSAKEN, OR FORGOTTEN.

Persecuted, but not forsaken. 2 Cor. 4:9. See 1 Sam. 12 : 22.

Forsake me not, O Lord. Ps. 38 : 21.
The Lord thy God will not forsake thee. Deut. 31 : 6. See Jer. 51 : 5.

Wherefore dost thou forget us for ever, and forsake us so long time? Lam. 5 : 20.
O Israel, thou shalt not be forgotten of me. Is. 44 : 1. See 54 : 7.

Cast me not off in the time of old age; forsake me not when my strength faileth. When I am old and greyheaded, O God, forsake me not. Ps. 71 : 9, 18.

Even to your old age, and to hoar hairs will I carry you, and deliver you. Is. 46 : 4. I will never leave thee, nor forsake thee. Heb. 13 : 5.

I have been young, and now am old; yet have I not seen the righteous forsaken nor his seed begging bread. Ps. 37 : 25. For thou, Lord, hast not forsaken them that seek thee, 9 : 10.

Zion said, The Lord hath forsaken me, and my Lord hath forgotten me. Can a woman forget her sucking child? Yea, they may forget, yet will I not forget thee. Behold I have graven thee upon the palms of my hands; thy walls are continually before me. Is. 49 : 14-16. See Ps. 42 : 9; 106 : 4; Is. 44 : 21; Ps.

ESTABLISHED.

His heart is fixed, trusting in the Lord; his heart is established. Ps. 112 : 7, 8.

It is a good thing that the heart be established with (by) grace. Heb. 13 : 9. Rooted and grounded in love. Eph. 3 : 17. Rooted and built up in Him, and stablished in the faith. Col. 2 : 7.

I long to see you that I may impart to you some spiritual gift, to the end that ye may be established. Rom. 1 : 11.

He brought me up out of an horrible pit, out of the miry clay; and set my feet upon a rock, and established my goings. Ps. 40 : 2.

As ye have therefore received Christ Jesus the Lord, so walk in him, rooted and built upin him, and established in the faith. Col. 2 : 7.

Establish thou the righteous. Ps. 7 : 9

Believe in the Lord, so shall ye be established. 2 Chrn. 20 : 20. If ye believe not, ye shall not be established. Is. 7 : 9.

Now he which establisheth us, is God. 2 Cor. 1 : 21.

The God of all grace, after ye have suffered a while, make you perfect, stablish, strengthen, settle you. 1 Pet. 5 : 10. The Lord is faithful who shall stablish you.

STEADFAST.

Hezekiah clave to the Lord, and departed not from following him. 2 Kings, 18 : 6.

I have opened my mouth unto the Lord, and I cannot go back. Jud. 11 : 35.

If any man draw back, my soul shall have no pleasure in him. Heb. 10 : 35.

We are not of them who draw back unto perdition; but of them that believe to the saving of the soul. Heb. 10 : 39.

No man, having put his hand to the plough, and looking back, is fit for the kingdom of God. Lu. 9 : 62.

Seeing that we have a great High Priest that is passed into the heavens, Jesus, the Son of God, let us hold fast the profession Heb. 4 : 14, of our faith without wavering. Heb. 4 : 14 ; 10 : 23. For we are become partakers of (with) Christ, if we hold fast the beginning of our confidence firm unto the end. 3 : 14.

Beware lest ye being led away with the error of the wicked, fall from your own steadfastness. 2 Pet. 3 : 17. Remember Lot's wife. Lu. 17:32. Wherefore take unto you the whole armor of God, that ye may be able to withstand in the evil day, and, having done all to stand. Eph. 6:13. See Matt. 10 : 22 ; Gal. 5 : 1 ; Phil. 4 : 1 ; 1 Pet. 5 : 8, 9.

FORWARD.

Speak unto the children of Israel, that they go forward. Ex. 14 : 25.

Leaving the principles of the devotion of Christ, let us go on unto perfection. Heb. 6 : 1.

Grow in grace, and in the knowledge of our Lord and Saviour Jesus Christ. 2 Pet. 3 : 18.

Forgetting those things which are behind, and reaching forth unto those things which are before, I press toward the mark for the prize of the high calling of God in Christ Jesus. Phil. 3 : 13, 14.

We thank God that your faith groweth exceedingly. 2 Thess. 1 : 3.

The Lord will perfect that which concerneth me. Ps 138 : 8.

He which hath begun a good work in you will perfect it until the day of Jesus Christ. Phil. 1 : 6.

The righteous shall hold on his way, and he that hath clean hands shall be stronger and stronger. Job 17 : 9.

The path of the just is as the shining light, that shineth more and more unto the perfect day. Prov. 4 : 18.

They go from strength to strength, every one of them in Zion appeareth before God. Ps. 84 : 7.

I KNOW WHOM I HAVE BELIEVED.

BY REV. W. H. PORTER, M.A.

I know not what may be my lot,
In palace grand, or lowly cot,
But humble though my home may be,
The King of Glory dwells with me.

CHORUS.
"For I know whom I have believed,
And am persuaded that He is able
To keep that which I've committed
Unto Him against that day."

I know not what may be my pain,
My grief, my loss, my joy, or gain,
But having Him my soul hath claimed,
The Christ of God, "I'm not ashamed."

Chorus—"For I know whom," etc.

I know not what fond friend may go
And leave me, or become my foe,
But having found the Friend I need,
He'll ever be my Friend indeed.

Chorus—"For I know whom," etc.

I know not what the way may be,
The time or place He'll come for me,
But little need I fear or care
How life may close, or when, or where.

Chorus—"For I know whom." etc.

INDEX.

	PAGE.
My Saviour	4
Longing after God	5
To Find God	6
To See God	7
To Know God	8
To Be near God	9
To Behold His Beauty and Glory	10
To Be With and Like Him	11
God's Mercy	12
The Forgiveness of Sin	13, 14
Justified	15, 17
Cleansed	18, 20
Peace	21, 22
Rest	23
Guidance	24
Christian Work	25, 28
God's Word Inspired	29
Spiritually Understood	30
Pure and Purifying, Enlightening	31
Sure, True, Right	32
The Unerring Standard, Life giving	33
Precious	34
Practical	35
Prayer	36
Strength	37
God's House	38
Trust in God	39

Kept	40, 41
A Mediator	42
Salvation	43
Mutual Love and Longings	44
Help in Trouble	45
Comfort for the Afflicted	46
Comfort	47
Comfort in Sorrow	48
Comfort to Mourners	49
Joy	50, 52
Joy in Sorrow	53
Rejoicing in Hope	54
Prayer	55-58
Love	59
Brotherly Love	60
Obedience	61, 62
Light	63
Provided For	64
Filled	65
Satisfied	66
Sanctified	67
Holiness	68
Christ's Second Coming	69, 70
God's Presence	71
God Sees	72
Backsliding	73
Returning	74
Upheld	75
Not Forsaken or Forgotten	76
Established	77
Steadfast	78
Forward	79
I Know Whom I Have Believed	80

www.ingramcontent.com/pod-product-compliance
Lightning Source LLC
Chambersburg PA
CBHW031606110426
42742CB00037B/1304